Walking
into the
Light

**A 28-Day Pilgrimage
for Advent or Anytime**

Chuck Sandy

WAYZGOOSE PRESS

Walking into the Light: A 28-Day Pilgrimage for Advent or Anytime
Copyright © 2016 by Chuck Sandy

Edited by Dorothy Zemach
Cover design by DJ Rogers

ISBN-13: 978-1-938757-30-3

TABLE OF CONTENTS

HOW YOU MIGHT
WANT TO USE THIS BOOK

If you've gotten ahold of this book, it probably means you're thinking of making some changes in your life. Or maybe you're just wanting to mark off a section of time and during this time to do things a little differently, a little more consciously. Perhaps you're just curious yet resistant to the idea of change. Or you might be someone who cringes just a little whenever you hear someone make reference to the Divine and talk too much about the Light. That's fine. All I'll ask of you is that you take the first steps and pay attention. The rest is all up to you.

Though this is a pilgrimage, it's important to note that not every pilgrimage requires travel. Some you can do right in your own home, right where you are, and maybe in terms of distance you'll go no further than the edges of your neighborhood. This is one of those stay-close-to-home pilgrimages; but even so it's a journey, and you can't take a journey without it changing you some.

On this 28-day journey, we'll be on the lookout every day for ways to better let the Divine shine through, while listening closely for calling, staying open to wonder and surprise, and experimenting with practices for traveling light and keeping it holy. Some days it will all come together. Other days it won't. We expect this. Though we're headed towards the mountain-tops, we're ready for the valleys. Though we long to walk in the light, we're ready for the darkest nights. That's the pilgrim life: Every day a new beginning; blessings always already on the way.

Although this book is designed on one level to coincide with the Christian Advent journey that begins on a Sunday four weeks before Christmas, takes us through some pretty dark times, and then has us celebrating the birth of the true Light on Christmas Day, this is a journey that can be taken anytime, in what some Christians call Ordinary Time. The world is full of darkness, and we're always called to walk through it towards the light, and we're always called to help others along the way. If you believe this much, then this book is for you.

Our pilgrimage begins with some first steps and concludes with some next steps. In between there are 28 way-marked days along the way. It would be easiest for you, especially if you are using the book in Advent season, to begin your journey on a Saturday and then start out on a Sunday. That will take you through four weeks, and then you'll take your onward steps on a Monday. That's easiest; but however you choose to use the book will be the right way for you.

Each day on this pilgrimage journey you're offered a practice, a photograph, a story, and some suggestions for further reading from the Christian tradition.

You're welcome to use this book in any way you wish. You might, for example, use the photographs as writing prompts for journaling, or you might find yourself wanting to write a little memoir after reading some of the stories I share. If you're not a writer, maybe you'll do some sketching, or perhaps you'll tell others your stories. You might like to just keep quiet and work through the book on your own, and that's okay, too. Still, I'll suggest that you somehow keep a record of what happens to you along the way. In most entries, I suggest a small change in perspective or a particular action you could take. If you do these things, then you'll probably want to know what effect this has on your life. Find a way to document this if you can. Then at the end, you'll be able to look at this map you created and see where you were when you started and compare that to where you got to.

And if you'd like to share stories with me or just get connected, you could follow me on Twitter, where I am @chucksandy and where I'll no doubt be sharing more.

1st Steps

BEGIN AGAIN

Let everything happen to you
Beauty and terror
Just keep going
No feeling is final
> ~ Rainer Maria Rilke

Let's say you've stepped into a difficult day. Maybe you've received news that's not easy to process. Perhaps a shadow has crossed your consciousness: a worry, a fear, a sadness. Or let's say you've stepped into a beautiful day. You're deep in the flow, and every joy is yours.

Earlier this week, I stepped into that deep-in-the-flow day full of joy. The other morning I stepped into that shadowy day. Tomorrow, who knows what will come? It could be beauty. It could be terror. There could be light. There might be darkness. It all comes, and yet nothing ever stays for long.

You do not have to wait until tomorrow to begin again. You do not have to wait even one more moment. You could begin again right now. Take one step in a new direction. Now take another. Now keep going and don't stop. Not now, anyway.

No matter where you are on the journey today, no matter how you're feeling right now, just keep going. Even if it feels like you can't go on, you can. Take a step. Then take another one. That first step might be a deep breath. It might be some words you write. It might be a walk through the shadows and into the light. Let everything happen. Keep going until you feel better, and on this pilgrim journey pay attention to the things that cross your consciousness. They very well might be the very things you need to know. You can begin quietly again.

Start now.

1st Sunday

LIGHT A CANDLE. REIGNITE HOPE.

"Bᴜᴛ ᴛʜᴀᴛ'ꜱ ᴊᴜꜱᴛ ᴀ ᴄʀᴀᴢʏ ᴅʀᴇᴀᴍ," ꜱɪɢʜᴇᴅ ᴍʏ ꜰʀɪᴇɴᴅ. "Nobody's going to give me a scholarship," said the woman. "Maybe I should give up on love," cried the heartbroken man. "We're not going to get through this!" shouted my son as we passed through the storm. It's hard enough to believe, dream, hope, and wait on the best days. It's much harder when we meet the disappointments, heartbreaks, and setbacks we always encounter. Yet "we must wait," writes Dietrich Bonhoeffer, "for the greatest, most profound, tenderest things."

He goes on to say that these things don't happen "in the storm" but because of it and then "according to the divine laws of sprouting, growing, and becoming." Experience bears this out. That dream wasn't just crazy. It was really crazy. A community made it work. Someone did give that woman a scholarship, but it was to study something different. That became her passion. The heartbroken man did find love, but it appeared where least expected. And that storm, well, we rode it out and it took us home. That's how it works. You're about to give up just when you shouldn't. Then you let go of the predefined – and that sets Hope free.

Today as we begin our journey towards Christmas, choose an unrealized dream from your own life, say a prayer, and light a candle. Consider that a radical act which says, "I'm reigniting hope here." Then keep your eyes open. Dreams get realized in ways we can't imagine, and that's what Christmas is about.

Have Hope.

Read Isaiah 9.2 and Romans 13: 11-14

1st Monday

TAKE ONE STEP FORWARD.
CONQUER A FEAR.

"I'M NOT STRONG ENOUGH TO GET THROUGH THIS," CONfessed the patient. "I don't even know how to begin again," sighed the dropout. "I'll never get over that hill," said the pilgrim. Fear had them in its grip. I know. I was all three of those people.

One day my teacher said, "Step away from that fear and into what you most hope for. The door's open. I can't tell you what you'll find when you do, but I can promise you it will be better than living in fear." And he was right. Yet, it's a lesson I've had to learn over and over again, as all of us do.

Think of this Advent journey as an open door that you've been invited to walk through. I can't tell you what you'll find or show you the way. I can only tell you that every time I've taken this step, my experience has echoed Thomas Merton's, who writes: "I was not sure where I was going, and I could not see what I would do when I got there. But You saw further and clearer than I, and You opened the seas before my ship, whose track led me across the waters to a place I had never dreamed of, and which you were even then preparing to be my rescue and my shelter and my home."

So why am I still sometimes afraid? I confess – I am. But I'm taking a step, here. Take one, too. This is a radical act which says, " I am not scared here." As you step, say those words. If you can't manage that, let your action speak. We're pushing the darkness back. We're taking a step. Tomorrow we'll take another.

Read Hebrews 11 and Psalm 72

1st Tuesday

GET QUIET. LOOK AND SEE. LISTEN AND HEAR.

"WHAT ARE YOU DOING?" ASKED MY THEN 8-YEAR-old son as he walked into my study to find me sitting there all serious-like, with my eyes closed. "I'm praying," I answer. "Why aren't you moving your mouth?" he asks. "Because this is contemplative prayer. It's like meditation," I say. "What's meditation?" he asks. "Well, you empty your mind, and..."

Then he excitedly says, "Let's try it together! The first one who has a thought is out. Go!" One second later he says, "Okay, I'm out," and we both laugh hard.

The joy that rose up between us then was divine. Though we didn't achieve anything close to a contemplative state, we got something even better. We were present in the moment and open to its unfolding, and maybe that's the very place where we're most likely to meet God: in the moment, in the unexpected, in the unfolding. And in my case on that day, in the laughter. That's what Advent asks of us: to be present, open, aware, and awake. This is not easy. "Now we will count to twelve / and we will all keep still," writes Pablo Neruda. Try that. Go!

Like my young son, you'll probably find this difficult at first. I did and still do. That's why every Advent I make this practice a conscious part of my every day. Sometimes I sit by a window, looking out at what's there, and let the view quiet me. Other times I walk through what's there and let my footsteps quiet me. Either way, the stillness that unfolds in the space that stillness creates begins to speak: Birds sing; a breeze moves through the trees; a leaf falls. Joy rises. Christmas comes closer. Now, it's important to note that I don't know anything much, but I will tell you this: It's been my experience that if you make space for the Divine to enter, it will. Stillness is the invitation. Even the intention to be still is sometimes enough. If you've walked through Advent's door and taken a step towards Hope, now try to be quiet.

Look and See. Listen and Hear. May what's revealed be what you need.

Read Mark 7:35 and Psalm 26

1st Wednesday

HAVE FAITH IN WHAT YOU HOPE
FOR BUT CAN'T YET SEE

SOME DAYS JUST GO ON AND ON. SOME TASKS SEEM pointless. We ask ourselves, "Why am I doing this?" We wonder where it's all leading. We'd like to quit, but we can't. Take a step, someone says. Keep your eyes open, says another. We smile and thank them, but on days like this, advice like that makes us cringe.

One day on the Camino de Santiago pilgrimage, I walked 18 kilometers alone along a flat gravel path through post-harvest fields. There wasn't much to see, no place to rest, and nothing to do except keep going. Then I saw this sign: *Don't quit before the miracle.* Ha! What miracle could that be? I thought, and trudged on.

All at once the sun came out, the brown fields glowed golden, and the gravel path began to glitter like it was made of diamonds. Then the sun set, one bright star came out, and I followed it downhill to a village where friends were waiting to greet me. Thank God some days end like that, because most don't.

Eight hours into a 12-hour flight recently, I thought about that. I thought of the struggles so many friends are facing, of those days when it's pretty hard to believe what we're doing has meaning and where we're headed is good. Clearly there are things we just have to get through, times when all we can manage is to keep moving forward with as much hope as we can muster and not give up.

The Advent journey reminds us that this is worth doing. It's all about hard travel, difficult times, and miracles happening to unlikely people in unlikely places. Let's say you're or a pilgrim on a journey, a shepherd out in the field, or more likely someone at the beginning, the middle, or the end of a long day, and you're tired. Be strong and take heart. This story is about you. Have faith in what you hope for but can't yet see.

And get some rest. We've got a long way to go.

Read Matthew 4:16 and Psalm 31

1st Thursday

DO SOMETHING TO MAKE
THE WORLD HOSPITABLE AGAIN

T HERE ARE DAYS WHEN IT'S ESPECIALLY IMPORTANT to interrupt the narrative of despair. Today has been such a day. That's why I want to tell you a story.

Not long ago I was grocery shopping with my parents. On the drive in, we heard devastating news. There'd been another mass shooting. My father switches the radio off and we ride along in silence. What is there to say? A few minutes later, we're getting out of the car in front of the supermarket when this woman comes rushing over with her arms flung open wide. "Oh, my God!" she cries out. "It's so good to see you!" Not missing a beat, my mother smiles her warmest smile and says, "It's so good to see you too!" Then they hug as if they're long-lost sisters.

After a while, the woman steps back, looks at my mother, and says, "I really needed that. Thank you." My mother smiles and says, "Me, too. Thank you." They exchange a few more words, and then the woman's gone. "Who was that?" I ask, thinking this was someone from my parents' church or maybe some distant cousin. "I have no idea," says my mother, "but it seemed like she really needed a hug, so why not?" Yes, why not? In dangerous times, every hug matters.

We cannot sit and wait for light to return to the world. In darkest winter, we must provide light for one another. As Parker Palmer writes, "A stranger's act of kindness can makes the world seem hospitable again."

Do that.

Read John 13: 33-45 and Psalm 136

1st Friday

OFFER A TURNING POINT

Dᴜʀɪɴɢ ᴀ ʀᴇᴄᴇɴᴛ Aᴅᴠᴇɴᴛ sᴇᴀsᴏɴ, ᴀ ʟɪᴛᴛʟᴇ ɢɪʀʟ ɪɴ our church lit a candle for Hope and then the sweet voices of the children's choir sang, "Light one candle for Hope, one bright candle for Hope. He brings Hope to everyone. He comes. He comes." Their faces aglow in candlelight made the night bright. That's the world we want.

Yet after that service I walked out into a world so in need of Hope that it almost broke my heart. This is the world we live in.

How do we reconcile that? How can we turn things around? Perhaps the only way is one heart, one mind, one soul at a time – or more practically: one kindness, one meal, one gesture of love at a time. I'm not talking about winning souls for Christ here; I'm talking about being the hands and feet and arms of Christ in whatever ways our little lives allow.

Our world is full of people who are one day away from giving up. How can we show them that they shouldn't? How can we encourage them to take another step? When things seem hopeless, it's especially important to remember that it doesn't take much. In fact, Corrie ten Boom writes that it's most "often a small, almost unconscious event that makes a turning point" in someone's life.

Recently for me it's been a son's sweet smile, a friend's trust, and a stranger's encouragement. One day it was an unexpected gift received via email and later seeing a kindness offered and received. Another day it was a smile from an old man and a pat on the back. Sometimes it's being seen and acknowledged, heard and comforted, shown love and forgiven. Other times, maybe it's you who's offered such grace, and what sets it in motion is gratitude.

These little lights in the darkness are nothing small, and they're not just turning points. These are the candles we light for Hope, and whenever we offer or accept them, He comes, He comes.

Read: Matthew 25:11 and Galatians 6:2

1st Saturday

SHARE THE SWEETNESS

"THESE ARE SO SWEET. TASTE. YOU'LL SEE," SAYS THE old farmer. Then he takes my hand in his and drops two candies in it. His smile is full of gold. "You are my friend forever. Don't forget it!" Then he gets in his truck, waves, and drives off. I stand there looking at the candies in my hand. Who had I just met on this lonely road? I put one of the candies in my mouth, the other in my pocket, and walked on.

Later that evening, a man comes to sit beside me in the village square. "Want half?" he asks, as he unwraps a sandwich. I tell him I'm good, but he's pretty insistent. He cuts the sandwich in half, hands me my share, and we eat in a companionable silence. Wanting to give him something, I pull out the piece of candy and put it in his hand. He looks at it and says, "The old farmer, right? He gave me some, too." He pauses and says, "Then, he gave me our sandwich." I laugh out loud and call it a funny coincidence. "It's no coincidence," he says. "It's a freaking miracle! That's what that old farmer does, man. He shares the sweetness and channels the Friend." That's what you do too, I tell him. He puts that piece of candy in his pocket – maybe for later, maybe to share with someone else further along the road – and says, "You do that too, man."

My new friend reaches into his bag, pulls out a bottle of wine, and takes a drink. Then he passes it to me and says, "I've been thinking of those lines from Matthew. You know those, right? 'I was hungry and you gave me something to eat. I was thirsty and you gave me something to drink. I was a stranger and you gave me ... something sweet.'"

I have some of the wine and tell him I know what he means. "Do you really?" he asks. "I think I do," I say. "Then you know we just took communion together, brother. Come on, let's go." When I put my pack back on, I found that something had shifted. My load felt lighter. I was no longer tired. I'd been fed.

In this dark Advent season, keep your eyes open for The Friend. Lighten the load for others by sharing His sweetness.

Read Matthew 25: 35 and Psalm 34: 8

2nd Sunday

LIGHT A CANDLE FOR HAPPENING

"MAY THE CANDLE YOU LIGHT FOR HOPE TURN YOUR hopes into happenings," wrote a friend. I really like that: *turn your hopes into happenings*. But how does one do that? Maybe the answer is in the verb. Turn: as in a new direction. Turn: as in turn around. Sometimes that's all it takes. But where to start?

A teacher I love suggests first looking carefully at one area of your life that doesn't seem to be working out very well. What are you doing, and how are you doing it? If you're a list maker, make a list. If you're a writer, write descriptions. If you're more visual, make sketches. Whatever you do, look.

Then find one small change you can make and make it. Now look again. What's happening now? Are things getting better? Great. Keep going and pay attention to what's changing. No? Go back and change something else. Then do it again.

By consciously and continually making small changes, we change. We also begin to see that making small changes can lead to transformation, and that the power to turn things around is not only within reach, it's within us. In today's Advent readings, we encounter John the Baptist out in the wilderness calling us to turn back, to turn around, to head off in a new direction, and by doing so, to see things differently, to have a change of heart, to be heartened and to have hope.

But don't just stand around hoping, John says. Make room for Hope by taking action. Though the darkness is being pushed back, you've got to do your part and prepare the way. Take a step. Turn around. Make a change. Do what's needed to turn your hopes into happenings. You not only have the right; you've been called.

Read Isaiah 40: 1-11 and Mark 1: 1-8

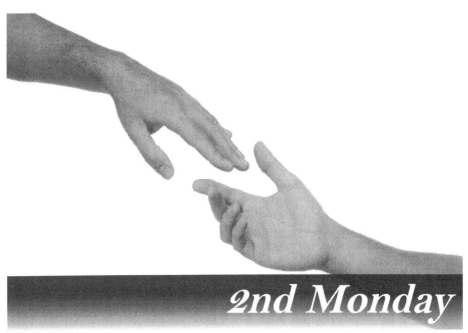

2nd Monday

DON'T BE AFRAID OF STRANGERS

"WHAT ARE YOU LOOKING FOR? SIGNS AND MIRA-cles?" asked the man with feathers in his hair as he approached me. I hadn't done anything to prompt this question. I was just a guy walking the Camino. I take a step back.

"Don't be afraid, brother."

I tell him I'm not, but the hairs on the back of my neck are standing up. This man doesn't look like a pilgrim. I take another step back. He comes closer and says, "Don't be discouraged. Just keep your eyes open, okay? Especially when you're feeling cold and tired, like you can't go on no more."

I'm thinking maybe I should run.

He says, "That's when the inner peace comes, brother," he says. "Once you stop fighting the war inside you…"

I still had a few kilometers to walk and there wasn't much daylight left. I mumbled my thanks and hurried off. Who was this guy, and why was I so scared of him? Just another voice in the wilderness. It started to rain, and the wind picked up. Then, night came on.

Let's say you're a shepherd out in the fields. Or you're a young woman sitting alone in her room. Or you're a fisherman, and somebody says, "Come, follow me." Would you? Would you even listen? The last stretch of the day's journey is a long steep hill, and I'm wet, cold, and exhausted. I'm not sure I'm strong enough to make it, but I do. That's when I see the message.

It says: "Soon the sun will make this writing disappear and fade away, and so it goes with your fear, tiredness, and pain. So keep in mind that when you are sore and feel like you can't go on no more, that inner peace comes after the war within. So walk strong my friend and remember … The wetness will always dry, the chill will always pass, and after the cold you will always find warmth."

I wished then I had at least been nicer to that guy. In fact, I wished I could go back and hug that man with feathers in his hair.

Read Deuteronomy 10:19 and Malachi 3:1-5

2nd Tuesday

BE A WITNESS

CROSSING MY US UNIVERSITY CAMPUS IN 1980, I WIT-nessed two men screaming at an international student from the Middle East while two others held his arms. A crowd gathered and closed in. Violence seemed imminent. Then, I saw my teacher move forward. His arms open. His face full of peace.

He approached the angry men and said something. Then he wrapped his arms around them and said some more. They let the boy go, and walked away. The crowd dispersed. The boy collapsed in tears. My teacher picked him up and held that boy in his arms. Love won.

Not that long ago, I was in a restaurant with my father when we heard the loud angry voice of the manager shout "Your kind is not welcome here" to a man who was trying not to cry. We did not know this man, but my father walked over and put his arm around him. "This is my friend," my father calmly told the manager. Peace prevailed.

The other day I was in a Dollar Store. A heavily tattooed teenaged girl came slouching in. "We've got security cameras," said the cashier. "Watch yourself." The girl glared. Just then an elderly woman smiled at the girl and said, "Never mind her. Could you help me with this bag?" As the girl reached to take it, the old woman said, "I love your tattoos. I've been thinking of getting one. Do you think I should?" "Seriously?" the girl asked. "You never know," said the woman. Then they both laughed. "You're so beautiful," the old woman said. "Really?" said the girl. "Thank you." As she walked off, her slouch was gone. Gentleness triumphed.

In these dark times, maybe it's more important than ever to shine some light on what's good. That's all I'm doing here. Be a witness.

Read Mark 16:15 and Acts 1:8

2nd Wednesday

SET A MIRACLE IN MOTION

When I was a painfully shy little boy, a teacher who saw that I was hiding behind a book came over, pulled up a little chair, and asked what I was reading. I don't remember the book, but I'll never forget how she looked right into me and asked, "Did you know that you have the most beautiful blue eyes?"

I didn't know that, but before I could say so, she said, "You don't have to be like anyone else, you know. You can be anything you want to be." I hadn't known that either, so when I grew up I became a teacher.

There's more to the story, of course. There always is, but I think that's how miracles work: someone's pain gets met at the exact point of need and is healed with love. Sometimes it's instantaneous. Most times it takes a good long while.

Always Love is what sets the miracle in motion.

You might think that doesn't quite add up, and that's ok: it doesn't need to add up. "A miracle," writes Frederick Buchner, "is when the whole is greater than the sum of its parts. A miracle is when one plus one equals a thousand." The Christmas story is full of miracles like that.

So are our lives. I'm really not trying to convince you of anything here, but what if the words that come out of our mouths today, combined with the meditations of our hearts right now, were enough to set miracles in motion?

Maybe that's worth thinking about and acting upon.

Read Isaiah 50:4 and Mark 11:24

2nd Thursday

THROW A PARTY.
GLADDEN SOME HEARTS.

J ESUS LOVED A GOOD PARTY. HE ATE AND DRANK HIS WAY through the gospels, making His table a place of radical welcome and any party He was at a feast of joy and celebration. More wine? Sure, let me take care of that. Not enough food? Look again. Dinner with you? See you tonight. I know where you live.

Weddings, parties with friends, meals shared in the good company of the sort of people others shunned, family gatherings, whatever: Jesus was there to enjoy himself and provide the entertainment. Hey, did I tell you the one about the two brothers? Have you heard the one about the Great Banquet? I've got some stories to tell you, but first go get some more people.

The ones that were invited haven't turned up, and I've ordered the full course.

No, you take my place. I'll sit over there. This is fine. What's the kingdom of God like? It's a party that everyone's welcome to join. Pass the bread, would you? Stories get told, laughter gets shared, strangers become friends, love deepens, and somewhere between the breaking of the bread and the last shared spoonful of dessert wine, a light gets lit that sees you all through the dark nights.

Life's a banquet if you make it one, and everyone's welcome. Advent is a great time to throw a party and celebrate the coming Light.

Go ahead and do that. Gladden some hearts.

Read Hebrews 13:2 and Luke 14: 15-24

2nd Friday

STOP STRUGGLING

My 84-year-old father, who is completely deaf in one ear and has considerable hearing loss in the other ear, used to be famous for saying, "I hear all I need to hear. But I have an excuse. What's yours?" Well, I don't have one, but for much of my life, you could blame my big ego for blocking out the uncomfortable truth about myself and the way I was living. "What!?" I'd say. "What do you mean? Don't you understand that..." And of course those are fighting words.

My pride, my ego, all the half-truths I told and worked so hard to turn into a whole, blinded me – and defending who I was almost killed me. Why did I struggle so much and fight so hard and refuse to listen?

Well because deep down I realized that really listening would force me into having to make a change, and who wants to do that, really? Change is hard.

Fortunately, I have a dear friend who's never given up on me, someone who has always told me the truth about myself, even as I actively fought against it. Not some version of the truth, but the actual truth.

One day I finally had to listen because I'd fallen so hard I had no idea how to get up. That day when I least deserved it, my friend reached out, picked me up, and said, "Come on, let's go. It's going to be okay. I love you," and we went off in another direction. Though I'd like to tell you that this act of grace all at once changed everything about me, it didn't. The process is ongoing. Still, I'm listening better and trying harder. I'm every day more grateful for this loving friend.

Meanwhile out in the wilderness, John the Baptist is saying, "Listen up, people. You've got to change the way you're living. I know this is hard to hear, so I'm going to keep saying it until you're ready to listen because this is what love does. It tells the truth."
People ask John, "Who are you?"

"Me? I'm just a voice," says John, "and all I'm doing is getting you ready for what's coming: the Love that will reach out an offered hand and say, *Come on, let's go. It's going to be okay. I love you.*

Read Isaiah 40:3 and Matthew 3: 1-17

2nd Saturday

BE HOSPITABLE

I WAS IN AN INTERNATIONAL AIRPORT RECENTLY, WAIT-
ing for the flight that would take me from the country
I was born in to the country I now call home. With
some hours to kill, I made my way to the gate and sat
down in the waiting area.

Looking around me, I saw travelers from everywhere
doing their best to make themselves comfortable. I
saw families with children, couples, solo travelers, and
business people. Many of these people were dressed
in ways that made it seem like they might be from
somewhere else – but who can say, really? Not me.

An older man dressed in a dark suit walked up and sat across from me. Soon he was joined by a woman in a beautiful long red dress, her hair covered in a matching veil. The man caught my eye, smiled, and asked if he was at the right gate. I assured him he was. "We're going to visit my wife's sister. She's married to a Japanese man," he explained. His wife smiled. "We're Americans," he said.

As the man and I talked about the long flight to Tokyo, his wife unwrapped a package of cookies and offered me one. It was delicious.

Meanwhile on the big TV screen above us, the news was showing boat after boat overloaded with people on a dangerous journey to Greece. Volunteers met them with a bottle of water and a blanket. Meanwhile, other refugees were finally landing in Toronto. A mother lifted a child into her arms. An old woman kissed the ground.

Then on the screen came a man using dark words to stoke fear of the other. They don't speak our language, he was saying. They don't know our ways. They are not like us. We have to stand together in unity against them, he said. We have to unify. This is the new reality, he said. The TV newscaster nodded.

I looked around me. I saw the couple I'd spoken with falling asleep against each other. I saw the families, the children, the single travelers, and the business-people. All we wanted was to get somewhere else. All I wanted was to go home.

Over in Bethlehem, a poor couple arrive exhausted well past nightfall. The woman is heavy with child. All they want is a decent place where she can give birth. Again and again, they get turned away. No one except the woman herself realizes that she's carrying the light of the world within her. Many haven't realized this yet. And yet so many who claim to have understood continue their work to divide us.

Out in the wilderness, John the Baptist is calling us to change our ways. Listen. We do not need to discover a new unity or a new reality. In this dark world, "what we have to recover is our original unity," writes Merton. "My dear brothers (and sisters) we are already one," he writes. "But we imagine that we are not."

Let's not just imagine that we are. Let's act upon it by being hospitable to others.

Read Hebrews 13:1-2 and Luke 2:7

3rd Sunday

LIGHT A CANDLE FOR JOY –
NO MATTER WHAT

There's a poem by Rumi that I love. It goes like this:

> *This being human is a guest house.*
> *Every morning a new arrival: A joy, a depression,*
>   *a meanness,*
> *some momentary awareness comes as an unexpected visitor.*
>
> *Welcome and entertain them all – even if they're a crowd*
>   *of sorrows,*
> *who violently sweep your house and take all your furniture,*
> *still, treat each guest well. They may be preparing you*
>   *for some new delight.*

The dark thought, the shame, the malice, meet
them with laughter.

Be grateful for whoever comes. Each has been sent
as a guide from beyond.

What Rumi means is pretty much what the Apostle Paul means when he advises us to rejoice always no matter what. To the rational mind, it sounds like pure foolishness, but then there's nothing rational about joy. Sometimes joy arrives in the form of heartbreak, dressed up as hardship, disguised as a journey you'd rather not take, wrapped up as a child born in what looks like poverty. When it does, you're tempted to ask, What's up with that? Then you look again, and it turns out that what you thought of as disaster is opening the way to the good news you've been promised all along.

This is one of the things I love about the lead-up to the Christmas story, with its young couple on a difficult journey through the darkness. What looks like a soap opera you don't have to watch all the way through because you can guess how it ends has a brilliant twist. That wasn't disaster; it was incredible joy. Well, that could be anyone's story, couldn't it? And maybe that's the point. So open the door to whoever's there and be grateful for what is, says Rumi. Rejoice always and anyway, says Paul. "Don't be afraid," says the voice in the night. "I bring you good news." Just when you think it can't get any worse, it gets better than you've ever allowed yourself to imagine.

These things happen. They could happen to you.

Read Isaiah 61:1 and Thessalonians 5:16-24

3rd Monday

GIVE GOOD GIFTS

Growing up, I never thought of my family as poor. I thought of us as happy. Still, my father had three jobs, my mother had two, and though there was always enough, there wasn't too much else. Even so, my parents shared what there was with neighbors who had far less.

One Christmas season when I was around 10, my father took me with him to buy gifts for the children of a family whose father had vanished. When we got to the store, I immediately saw something I wanted and pointed it out to my Dad. "Think about that later," my father said. "Now, go find something nice for X." I slouched off on my own and my father went in a different direction to look for gifts for the other kids.

I was not happy.

X was a boy in my class whom I didn't like much, so I really didn't want to get him anything. However, my real concern was that choosing something nice for him might mean less for me. That's why I finally selected the crappy little toy I did. When I handed this to my Dad, he asked, "Would you be happy with this?" I admitted I wouldn't. "Then go get that thing you wanted, and we'll give that to X." I was upset. "What about me?" The look on my father's face told me I'd asked the wrong question. I went and got that good gift for X.

Later, we met X's mom in a parking lot. As I waited in the car, my father gave her the gifts we'd gotten for her children. She broke into tears and hugged my Dad. When he got back in the car, he said, "You can never tell anyone about this." Though I promised I wouldn't, forty some years later I'm breaking that promise, and not only because I'm still ashamed of the way I acted that day.

A fitting end to the story might be that on Christmas morning I got the crappy gift I'd tried to give my classmate, but that's not what happened. That day, I found my father had gotten that same gift for me, too. When I thanked him, he said, "Doesn't your father always gives you good gifts?" and it's taken me almost all these long years to understand just how good those good gifts are.

Out in the wilderness John the Baptist is giving practical advice: "Whoever has two coats should give one to the person who doesn't have any. Whoever has food should share it, too." It's pretty clear: We're called to do more than share nice stories and good feelings. We're called to give good gifts to each other because we ourselves who deserve so little have been given so much.

Read James 1:27 and Luke 3:11

3rd Tuesday

BE A BUILDER

W HEN I WAS NO MORE THAN A TODDLER, MY Uncle Lee gave me a plastic hammer for Christmas. Or maybe it was my parents who did. I don't remember. What everyone remembers is that I walked around saying, "I have a hammer. I can build a house." When my mother reminded me of this last week, she said something like, "You've always believed you could do anything."

I gently told her this was not true. What I wanted to say back then but couldn't yet express was that I admired Lee: a carpenter who, with the right tools, could take what looked like a pile of nothing and turn it into a beautiful house.

Lee was not an attractive man, nor a leader in any conventional sense. Yet with his goofy smile, unassuming manner, and down-to-earth goodness, Lee made everyone around him feel not just glad to be there, but also worthy and essential. When he passed away, I heard someone say, "That man was Christ's brother."

At the time, I thought that was an odd thing to say. Was this because Jesus was a carpenter too? That's what I thought then, but since then I've met many like Lee along the way: people from all over the world and from every background who shine with His light. Though they often think they're small, they're not. Almost always these are people who are completely unaware of how bright their light is, so I've taken it upon myself to tell them so – especially when I see them struggling.

Not long ago I was talking with a friend who was going through some very hard times. At some point in the long conversation, mostly about her troubles, she asked me why I was drawn to her. At this moment the conversation could have gone in a number of different directions, so I told her: It's because I see God at work in you and the work you do. It's so very important, and so are you. That just about floored her. She was quiet for a while before she asked if I really thought what I'd just told her was true. I assured her I was telling the truth. She had no idea. Now she does.

I don't have a hammer anymore, but I have a voice, and I'm not afraid to tell the truth. Still, this isn't about me. You have a voice, too. Please don't use it to quench the spirit. Instead, be a builder. Encourage each other with the truth.

That's one way to shine a light. I don't know much, but I've come to believe that in these dark advent times, there's probably no work that's more important nor easier to do than this.

Read Romans 14:9 and Matthew 5: 14-16

3rd Wednesday

ARISE AND SHINE

"THERE IS A LIGHT THAT SHINES IN THE DARKNESS, which is only visible there," writes Barbara Brown Taylor. It was good to be reminded of this on a particularly dark Wednesday. I'd woken up in a funk that felt pretty close to despair, and the gloomy weather wasn't helping. Nor did my morning reading, in which Thomas Merton was saying that…

> *Your brightness is my darkness.*
> *I know nothing of You and, by myself,*
> *I cannot even imagine how to go about knowing You.*
> *If I imagine You, I am mistaken.*
> *If I understand You, I am deluded.*
> *If I am conscious and certain I know You, I am crazy.*
> *The darkness is enough.*

Well, it certainly didn't feel like enough. Not today. How could I get through this?

That's when the phone rang. It was my mother telling me in her cheerful voice to "Arise and shine!" After our usual long conversation about this and that, I thought about her greeting. It comes from Isaiah:

"Arise, shine; for your light has come, And the glory of the Lord has risen upon you. Though darkness will cover the earth and deep darkness the peoples, the Lord will rise upon you and His glory will appear before you."

Arise. That's an action verb. I got up out of my chair. I stood up. I took a step. Then I put on my coat and went outside.

Later in this same passage, Isaiah says, "Lift up your eyes and look about you," and so I did. That's a doable action, too, and by taking it I began to find light in the most surprising places: on fallen leaves in the forest, in the depths of a pond, from behind gray clouds, reflected from a passing car, on a bird's wings. I stood there looking.

Then, all at once it happened: my heart throbbed and swelled with joy – just as it was promised. This is how it works, how even in the midst of despair, joy comes in and surprises you. It is like a child, waiting to step out of the darkness and be born within you.

Merton was right: Even the darkness is enough. Arise and shine.

Read Isaiah 60: 1-6 and Psalm 103

3rd Thursday

LEARN TO SAY NO

"WOULD YOU LIKE TO HELP US OUT?" MY FRIEND asks. "Well, if you can't find anyone else, I will," I answer. "Does that mean no?" he asks. I am trying to say no, but what I do next is pause a second before saying, "unless you really need me." He smiles and says "Okay, I'll give you a call." Sound familiar?

Even though we know we can't do everything there is to do, or be everything to everyone, we still find it hard to say no others, no to ourselves. Even when we realize that a yes now will lead to suffering later, we still say yes.

Why do we do this? Maybe it's because we hope that by postponing pain for some other time, we'll be able to make now better. But it doesn't. It never does. It just makes now worse, and usually makes later a big mess.

"Sure, I'll go there / do that / smoke this / eat that / do the job / say I love you," we say, though we know we shouldn't, though we don't really mean it. We want our pleasure now. We don't want to disappoint others. We don't want to let anyone down. Why do we do this?

In James 5:12 we're told to "Let your *yes* mean *yes* and your *no* mean *no*," or as Derek Silvers says, to say "Hell yes!" to the important people and things, and "No way" to all the rest, and just leave it at that.

Yet maybe there's a more loving way to say this, a way that honors who we are, who we're trying to become, and what we value. Maybe there's even room for the occasional *maybe* when we need time to think things through; but we should be sure to follow that *maybe* up with clear *yes* or *no* and not let any *maybe* linger for too long. That could be mistaken for a *yes*.

Wherever you are on your journey today, now is a good time to put this into practice, and to do it with love. Stay awake and focused for practice opportunities that might come your way. As the poet William Stafford writes, "It is important that awake people be awake or a breaking line may discourage them back to sleep; the signals we give – yes or no, or maybe – should be clear. The darkness around us is deep."

Take this seriously. The wrong *yes* might lead to a mess.

Read James 5:12 and Matthew 12:36-37

3rd Friday

LIGHTEN YOUR LOAD

W HEN I WALKED SEVERAL HUNDRED MILES OF THE Camino de Santiago pilgrimage route, I learned the importance of traveling light. On a journey like that, you're carrying everything you have on your back, so even an unnecessary few 100 grams can become a burden over the distance. Still, almost daily, instead of cutting back, I habitually added interesting brochures, souvenirs for myself and friends, and even books and notebooks to my backpack – not realizing how this added weight would eventually come to drag me down.

Then one morning, a couple of hundred miles into my walk, it happened: A hard uphill climb finally convinced me that I needed to lighten my load. As soon as I could, I tossed everything that wasn't essential. Some of it got left at a hostel give-away box. Some stuff I mailed home from the first post office I found. Still I needed to get rid of more, so out went everything that I could do without. Some of that stuff was hard to part with, but letting it go increased not just my walking speed but more essentially, it increased my joy on the journey.

I'd like to tell you that I didn't need to learn this lesson again, but I did: repeatedly, and not only on the trail. A year ago, I spent hours deleting computer files I no longer needed or which no longer represented who I am. Today I did that again. It was disheartening to see how much stuff I'd saved over the past year that was neither necessary nor helpful. Then, looking deeper at my life, I had to admit that the problem isn't too much stuff. The problem is me.

As often as I'd like to say no, I say yes. As much as I'd like to change, I often don't. Instead I hang on to habits and ways of thinking that drag me down. On this day late in Advent, I stood at the crossroads and took a long look. Then I asked for direction. The answer was pretty clear: It's time to part ways with the things in my life that are dragging me down.

Okay, then, but how? The memory of an even harder climb on the Camino floated into my mind. Even with my lighter pack, this stretch was too much. As I was struggling up, a man came along and offered to carry my bag.

At first I told him, "No thanks, I'm fine." But when he told me "There's no weakness in admitting you need help," I had to say it: "All right, then. I admit it. I need help." He took my burden from me and said, "Come on. Let's go. Walk with me."

Then, in addition to his own gear, he carried my pack to the top as I walked beside him. At the summit, he handed me my pack back, but he slowed his pace to stay with me until we reached the inn, and all along the way he told me stories and taught me songs. He even got me laughing.

Though he didn't have to do any of this, he did. That day this man offered me the strong back and gentle heart of Christ, and I couldn't thank him enough. "Don't mention it," he said. "My pleasure." How could I have forgotten?

All right then, Lord, I get it; and writing this helps me see that still now, on this very day, I need help. Please take this burden and walk with me. I look out into the distance. Just saying these words and remembering this helps. I can almost hear the man saying, "Give me what's heavy, and I'll give you rest. Come on. Let's go. Walk with me. I've got a story to tell you, and pretty soon you'll be laughing."

Read Jeremiah 6:16 and Matthew 11: 28-30

3rd Saturday

DON'T FEED THE FEARS

I HAVE A FRIEND WHO'S AFRAID OF EVERYTHING. IT DOES no good to tell her it's all in her head, because that's true. How did this happen? Perhaps like it began as it usually does, with words that injure, with lies that we come to believe are true.

"You'll never amount to anything," my father's 3rd grade teacher told him, and all his life he struggled with this thought. "Why would a person like you want to go to college?" asked my mother's father. Then he died and left her to wonder. "You won't survive as a writer," a teacher told me. "You'll never change," I overheard a man say to a colleague. "You're going to lose weight? Hah! That will never happen," one student said to another. "Isn't that just another one of your promises you'll never be able to keep, Chuck?" someone asked.

Unloving words like these unleash the darkness and lead to the fearful lies we tell ourselves. Lies like these: "No one understands me. Who would ever love me? I'll never succeed at ___. What if others find out I'm ___? I'll never ___. I'm not ___ enough." It's pretty easy to fill in those blanks. But please don't.

Those lies just feed the fear and fear is the enemy. Even when there are good reasons to feel afraid, fear has the power to immobilize. Maybe that's why every pronouncement in the Advent story is preceded by the words "Fear not" or "Don't be afraid." But always those words are followed by good news of promise and a next step.

It's not just "Everything's going to be great." It's always, here's an action to take: Listen. Stand up. Marry Mary. Go to Bethlehem. Call him Jesus. Follow the star.

Is there a practical application there? Maybe. So as I was talking with my friend today, I followed my "Don't be afraid" and my "Good things are going to happen" with an action plan: "Listen. Go to this website. Apply for that scholarship. Let's see what happens."

The truth is, I know what will happen: she'll get the scholarship because I have the ability to offer it and I will. After that, the rest is up to powers beyond me — powers I have great faith in, my Lord and Savior Jesus Christ. All I can do now is pray for her, and maybe I'll be shown a way to help her further. Maybe not. Perhaps just getting her started was enough for now. So though I can't say where this might take her, I believe it will be somewhere good, and already so does she. Already she's moving forward joyfully and is beginning to feel like she can do more than she thought she could do. This is where faith begins to take root.

While it would be easy to say this story about one person taking a step forward away from fear doesn't amount to much, we don't know that. The Gospels are full of stories about ordinary people like this, and maybe, just maybe, that's another practical application right there.

Good things could happen to you. You could help make them happen for someone else. Don't feed the fears.

Read Isaiah 41:10 and Luke 2:8-12

4th Sunday

LIGHT A CANDLE FOR LOVE

LET ME TELL YOU ANOTHER TRUE LOVE STORY. I KNOW a man who gave up everything he had upon learning – through the grapevine – that his high school sweetheart was pregnant. As she and her family had recently moved across country, he dropped out of college, gathered together what little money he had, got into his truck, and drove through the night to make things right.

When he finally arrives he asks, "Why didn't you tell me?" She says, "Because it's not your baby."

You'd think this would be the end of the story, but it's not. Life goes on, and like with most people's lives, theirs was the usual mix of joy and sorrow. New loves appeared, marriages happened, children arrived, and along the way they lost touch with each other.

Twenty-five years later the phone rings. "It's me," she says. "I need to talk to you." She's in a hospice dying of cancer. For a moment he hesitates, but then he says, "I'll be there soon."

'Soon' is a couple of days later. In that meantime, he goes back and forth in his mind, but he's been called. He knows he has to see her. He knows he has to go and make things right. Still he's not sure what he's going to say until he sees her, until she starts to speak. That's when he takes her hands in his and says, "Shhh. It's okay. I love you. I've always loved you, and I always will."

Something is released that allows her to pass away peacefully that night. That something sets the man free, too.

You'd think this would be the end of the story, but it's not because this is a love story, and this is what love is and does.

It forgives and heals. It never fails. It goes on. It's a lot like the Christmas story, when true love arrives and says, Here I am, but I'm not what you except. Then it grows up and the world does what the world always does. It tries to kill it, but it can't. Nothing can. Not even death.

True love is not a short story. It's the long journey that always was, always is, and always will be.

Read Luke 2:10 and 1 John 3:18

4th Monday

FEEL TIME EXPAND

At the edge of the darkening sky, there's something I can't quite remember. What was I doing out in the forest on a winter's night so long ago? Whatever it was, my father stands in the yard calling my name, and his voice shepherds me home.

Fifty-some years later, I stand by the pond listening on a day when time keeps slipping from the *right now* to the *what was* then out into the *not yet* and back again. I can almost feel time expanding. I'm 57 now. My father is 85. The other morning, we were talking on the phone about past Christmases.

"Do you remember when we..." and of course I do, but talking about it with him today brings it into the

present. Then he tells me about a Christmas when he was a boy when there wasn't much, and how grateful he is for all he has now.

Pretty soon we're discussing the young men in our family and our hopes for their futures. I'm about to close the call and get on with my day when my Dad says, "It's great to talk, but it's so important to listen." I ask him what he means.

"It must have been really quiet on that Christmas Eve when the shepherds were out standing in the field," he says. "Otherwise they wouldn't have been able to hear the angels." I'm not sure what to say, so I thank him for this thought and tell him how much I love him. "I appreciate that," he says. "I always have and I always will."

Then he hangs up, and I hear the clock ticking in my quiet house. I don't know how it works, but time is clearly a gift that's a whole lot less straightforward than we think. I don't even know what to think, but I feel it. Perhaps eternity isn't something we wait for; perhaps it's here right now without our beating heart. Later I'm standing by the pond listening, and what I hear are children's voices drifting down from the public elementary school in rural Japan where I live.

These Japanese children are singing a Christmas carol about a silent, holy night, and there I stand 7000 miles from the small town in NY where I was born.

I listen, and my Father's voice calls out into the solstice darkness.

"God enters into this moment – and this one, and this one – not simply to give us a glimpse of eternity," writes Jan Richardson, "but also to assure us that eternity is already at hand."

In these last few in-between days leading up to Christmas, may you have enough quiet in your life to listen and the ears to hear it. May time expand for you all the way into whatever is, was, and always will be.

Read Ecclesiastes 3:11 and Luke 2:8-14

4th Tuesday in Advent

BEGIN YET AGAIN

"LIFE IS CAMINO" BEGINS THE NOTE THAT'S BEEN LEFT for him to find. He picks it up and reads more: "Every morning you pack those few things you have and leave all that you love behind," it says. His eyes begin to water. It sounds like goodbye.

"You can't control, process, or hold on to what is given as a gift: Love," it says. He takes a deep breath and tries not to cry. Then he reads this: "But with an open heart, you can walk towards it again and again." That last sentence sounds like hope, so he folds the note, puts it in his wallet, and carries it with him as if it were a talisman.

Yet he understands nothing, not really. A few years later, he's by himself on a lonely path when the words come back to him: "Every morning you pack those few things you have and leave all that you love behind ... but with an open heart, you can walk towards it again and again."

The sun comes out. He's bathed in light. Something that feels like understanding goes off in his head, and he falls to his knees. That's how thankful he is. He thinks he's ready to begin again now, but before he does, he looks to make sure the note's still there. It isn't. Somewhere along the way, he lost it. The fact that he's saddened by this means he's still not ready. He understands nothing, not really. That's why he walks into the light still trapped in a story that, while true, is no longer serving him very well – because his version of it misses the point entirely.

A year will pass before he begins to understand. Then one morning it dawns on him: You can't walk into a new story while still telling yourself the same old story. No matter how you spin it, the old story's what's holding you back.

It's true. You can't control, process, or hold on to what has been given as a gift. Love. You've just got to trust it completely and have faith in the journey – no matter where it leads. No matter what. That's the day he packs his rucksack and head out for an all-day walk into whatever comes next.

He's almost home as the sun begins to set on this evening, but he stops on the path in the forest to let darkness fall around him. If he had a candle, he'd light it, he thinks, but he knows the path so well he could even close his eyes and still not stumble. That's why he decides to come home by another way – up the ridge into the deeper darkness and then down around past the elementary school and home. By now he's singing, some song he's just made up, and he because he feels like laughing, he does. How did I get here? he wonders. That old story got him there, he realizes.

The new one will get him home.

Whatever story has got ahold of you, make sure it's still working before you travel on. If it is, then fine. If not, then let it go.

Whatever you do and wherever you go, make sure you're walking towards Love and into a story that serves the Light.

Don't be afraid. Let go and take a new step. This is how you could begin again.

Read Isaiah 9:2-7 and Mark 4

4th Wednesday

WALK THROUGH IT

SOMEONE ASKED MY FATHER WHERE HE'D LIKE TO SPEND Christmas, and without missing a beat, he said 1965. He was joking, but in an Advent season when bad news keeps crashing into our days, it's tempting to become nostalgic about times in the past we remember as being happier and more peaceful.

Still, no matter how loudly the past calls us, we must make our home in the present and hold on to hope for tomorrow.

"But hang on a second, Chuck," a friend said. "How can you tell someone to hold onto hope when (this horrible thing) has happened?" I'll admit it's pretty hard sometimes, but I choose to believe that "Love is bigger than any of the grim, bleak shit the world can throw at us." That's a line from Anne Lamott I've copied out and put on a card above my desk.

There are days when I have to read it twice, because there really is a lot of grim, bleak shit being thrown at us. And this has always been true – even in that happily and probably selectively remembered past.

We never know what a day will bring. Still, though our hearts will break, heartbreak is not the final word. Our hearts also break open in ways that allow us to experience Love as we've never imagined we could. To get to that place, we have walk through this day and not give up. No matter what.

Anyone who claims that's easy to do is not telling the truth.

This is another reason I love the Christmas story. Just when it looks like things can't get much worse, they do; but then out of the utter darkness comes Hope in a form so helpless that it needs our nurturing and care. It's a baby crying in the night. What could be more surprising?

Listen to what's being born within you. Listen carefully, because sometimes that darkness is trying so hard to be louder that this quiet voice of love is pretty hard to hear. Are you listening? *Let Love break your heart open,* it coos. *There's reason to hope,* it cries.

Keep walking, it calls out. Then when it can speak, it makes one important promise: *It's worth walking through it all because Love is bigger than the world and its sorrows — so don't be afraid. I promise you this is true.*

This is the good news that allows us to say hooray for today and rejoice anyway, always and no matter what bleakness is being thrown across our path.

Don't worry about tomorrow. Just keep walking through today.

Read Isaiah 41:10 and Philippians 4:6-7
and Luke 2:2-20

4th Thursday

GIVE YOURSELF TO IT

"I LIVE MY LIFE IN WIDENING CIRCLES THAT REACH OUT across the world. I may not complete this last one, but I give myself to it," writes Rilke in *The Book of Hours.* That's what I've been doing and why.

A few months ago, I could barely make it up the hill to my house, but I took the first step and did. That one step led to half a million more on the Camino de Santiago. There were times I wasn't sure I could complete that journey, but while walking the Way, I learned that this wasn't really important, as long as I gave myself to it by making each step matter.

Five hundred kilometers later, I was standing in front of the cathedral in Santiago de Compostela, thinking,

"I could do more"; and yet I didn't just mean farther. I meant more. And I still mean more. I'll always mean more.

This past year, I thought I'd been plagued by health problems; but looking back I see how that opened ways to opportunity. Despite asthma attacks that almost killed me and a lingering heart problem, I've made several trips abroad and am just about to finish this book.

But this isn't about me. It's about you.

Let's say it's evening on the Way and the sun is setting. Somewhere beyond the next bend in the road is a well-lit city on a hill. Will you make it before nightfall? You can't say for sure. No one can.

And yet we have a choice. We could stop here and hope for the best, or we could head for the light. We could make each step matter. We could wake up while we still can. We could give ourselves to it. Maybe it's best to walk, while we have the light, while it's still today.

Read Ephesians 5:6-14 and John 12:35-36

4th Friday

BUILD A COMMUNITY OF TWO

IF YOU'RE READING THIS DURING ADVENT IN THE NORTH-ern Hemisphere, the darkest days have now past and Light is coming back to the world. No matter what season it is where you are now, know this: a fire has been lit. It's a strong, bright fire, but it needs constant kindling and attention. It needs to burn even brighter. How can we do this in a world that keeps reminding us of how dark it is?

It's simple.

A wood fire needs fuel, heat, and oxygen. The fire of the human spirit needs to be stoked with love, kindness, encouragement, and community. For those who have not seen the fire, for those whose fires have gone nearly out during the long night, even waking to face in the direction of the coming light might seem an impossible challenge. If they're not paying attention, they might miss it.

They might not have noticed the turning of the seasons. They may not have heard the good news you have been given to share. You never know who these people are, but surely you'll meet some on your path today. I can promise you that.

Be gentle with whomever you encounter today in this transitional time. Even the strongest are weakened by a harsh world. For the weakest, an unkind word, a discouraging remark, an oversight, or the smallest cruelty could be enough to extinguish their fire completely. You know that.

Go out of your way to be encouragement for someone downhearted. Reach out to those who need refueling. Accompany someone lonely. Build a community of two. Remind someone that they're not alone. Share some good news. Be a bringer of the light.

This isn't just encouragement. It's a lifeline.

Read Isaiah 9:2-7 and Psalm 43

4th Saturday

OFFER GRACE AND SERVE IT
TO THOSE IN NEED OF IT

IT DOESN'T MATTER WHO YOU ARE OR WHAT YOU BE-
lieve. It doesn't matter what path you're on or where
you are at this moment. Something is calling you.
Let's call this Love. Sometimes it calls out so clearly it almost knocks you down. Most often, though, it
whispers a quiet nudge into the center of your heart.

Listen.

One day I was standing in front of the cathedral in
Santiago de Compostela with a 20-euro note in my
hand, and I feel that nudge. When I look up, I see
a woman on crutches slowly climbing the hill in the
rain. Each step she takes looks more painful than

the last, and yet her face is full of jubilant awe. She's walked 700 kilometers on the Camino to get here, and she's alone.

What a shame no one is here to meet her at this moment of triumphant arrival, I think. And then I get nudged harder: But you're here, Chuck. I open my arms as she approaches and close them around her as she collapses into them. It's just the two of us. I'm hugging her tight as she weeps, and I'm saying, "It's okay, it's okay, I'm here. I'm here." Then a voice comes from my mouth, and it says, "I love you."

We pull back a bit and look into each other's eyes. It's not a pretty sight. Her glasses have been knocked askew. Snot is running from her nose. I'm sure I must look a sight as well. "I love you too," she sobs and we hug again. That's when I remember the 20-euro note in my hand. "I didn't know why I was carrying this until I met you," I say as I hand it to her. She looks at me. "Oh, my God!" she says. "I ran out of money yesterday and had nowhere to stay last night." She's crying harder. No, actually, we're both crying harder now. And yet there's this joyous feeling too.

Something wonderful is taking place in this moment, and we're a part of it. A crowd of pilgrims has gathered around us. They've seen what's happened. They know the story. Now we're all a part of it. Before long, this woman has a couple hundred euro, a place to stay, and a new family of friends helping her up the cathedral steps. "Hey, what's your name?" someone asks.

"My name is Grace," she says.

Of course her name is Grace. This is all about Grace. That's when I look up and see this sign we've been standing under all along. Angel, it says.

Listen. Something is calling you. Let's call it Love. May it be reborn in you each day. May is fill your heart on this very day. May it lead you to say yes to the Love that's calling you. Be an angel. Allow others to be an angel for you.

Read: 2 Corinthians 12:8-9 and 1 Peter 4:10

5th Sunday

LIGHT THE WAY

"MAY THE GIFT OF LOVE, HAPPINESS, PEACE, AND warmth be yours as you make a new start," reads the Christmas card I received from a friend in Iran. I'm so grateful for this friend who reached out across cultures and beliefs to send me this gift of encouragement. My life is full of good people like this, and today I sat quietly in a little church and thanked God for them all, one by one.

If you're reading this, you can be sure somehow that you were included on this long list – not by name, of course, but as someone who has read this book this far and shown me such grace. You are with me on the journey, and having such good company on the journey through the Advent darkness is a blessing that leaves me left me feeling more hopeful than ever.

Although the darkness around us is certainly deep, good traveling companions on the pilgrimage help us see a path through it – a path that's lit by good people of faith from all over the world. Although these people are not the Light itself, they reflect that Light. By doing so, each one along the way helps the next one still on the way.

I see how this works in our Christmas Eve candlelight service each year. We begin in darkness. Then we light one candle. From that candle, another candle is lit, then another, and from that one, another one. One by one, the light is passed to those still in darkness until there is no darkness in that place.

As you walk out into the world, you will encounter darkness and dangers. Our path is full of both miracles and monsters, angels in disguise, and demons too. Make no mistake about this; but there is a way through, and the way through needs to be peopled by the ordinary us offering grace, rest, light, and hope. No one will do this unless we do it for each other, and if you believe as I do that God is with us when we offer comfort to others, then you know what's possible.

The Light is here. It's always been here. It's never going away, and no darkness can squelch it. It's now up to us to pass it along. As we make a new start, as we tell each other our new stories, as we step out into the darkest night, let's be sure to light the way for each other. You are the light of the world, and you've been

called. If you've heard this call, if you've been asked to stay awake and guide others through the dangers and the darkness, then stay awake and pass on the peace the surpasses all understanding.

And as you continue on, may God grant you travel mercies already on the way.

In Christ's name I pray. Amen.

Read Ephesians 5:14 and Matthew 5:14-16

MAKE ONE DECISION AT A TIME

"I know there is no straight road
no straight road in this world
only a grand labyrinth of intersecting crossroads"
~ Federico Garcia Lorca

AFTER OUR LONG JOURNEY, WE ONCE AGAIN FIND OUR-
selves at a crossroads. This always happens. Which
way should we go? Should we continue on in the
direction we're going? Or maybe it's better to head
off in a new direction. Should we keep doing things
the way we've been doing them, or is now the right
time to really shake things up and make some further
changes? Questions like these used to freak me out so

badly that I'd wind up almost completely paralyzed. Jeez, I don't know. What if I make the wrong choice?

Then what?

One time when I was particularly stuck, I got some helpful advice. "Stay cool at the crossroads," a counselor said. "Stop, look, and ask for direction. Then do what's right, right then. You'll know."

But what if I mess up?

"You'll know that, too. That's another crossroads. One decision at a time, my friend. One decision at a time. Follow your inner compass. Redirect as needed."

I wrote that down so I wouldn't forget it. I often have. I sit here looking out my window on a rainy day with this book almost done, thinking maybe it's time for some redirection. Maybe it's time for something new.

Maybe that's where you are, too. If that's true for you, then stop, look, and listen. Then follow your inner compass. You can't get too lost if you always remember that you always begin again. It's always one decision at a time, my friend. One decision at a time.

May you have easy travels and a happy heart on the Way.

Read Jeremiah 6:16 and John 1:23 and Psalm 27

ABOUT THE AUTHOR

Chuck Sandy is a writer, teacher, motivational speaker, educational activist, and pilgrim. In 2014, he walked the Camino de Santiago pilgrimage route across northern Spain, and since then has been working to build pilgrim practices into his daily devotional life and everyday habits.

He's also founder of EdYOUfest, which reconnects what's inseparable by bringing communities of teachers and learners, doers, makers, and creators together in beautiful settings around the world for collaborative days of idea ignition; and a director of The International Teacher Development Institute (iTDi), which aims to better the world by helping teachers around the world become better educators. Chuck blogs on education, motivation, leadership, spirituality, and compassion for EFL Magazine and the iTDi Blog. Connect with Chuck on Twitter (@chucksandy) and follow him on Facebook (https://www.facebook.com/ChuckSandy).

29183790R00049

Printed in Poland
by Amazon Fulfillment
Poland Sp. z o.o., Wrocław